F**K VINTAGE AND F**K BUNTING

M.E. CROFT

PORTICO

INTRODUCTION

Modern culture is obsessed with trends. Every day we are bombarded with new and increasingly stupid things that we are told are fashionably 'hip', 'in' and 'hot'. We – *the people who have to swallow this nonsense* – get no say in this, it just happens and we are expected to go along with it. Well, no more, I say! Let's leave the past where it belongs and move on. Quickly.

F**k Vintage and F**k Bunting is your alternative antidote to the current national obsession with all things old-fashioned, trendy, vintage, old-school and retro. From the countless websites and bloggers that declare (inanely) 'tea cozys are in again', to the culture sections of newspapers telling us that 'retro' is the 'new old-school' and totally 'bang on-trend', like it means something. Why can't we all just live in the present and appreciate now for now's sake, huh?

This pocket-sized piece of present-day propaganda will entice you back into the warm embrace of the modern world and take you back to the future again (for the first time). Hopefully it will guide you back from the brink of rose-tinted madness and give you the confidence to tell all things vintage, retro and ridiculous to 'F**k off' back to where they belong – in the past.

'Let's do the Time Warp again.'
The Rocky Horror Picture Show

VINTAGE DEFINITION

Before we go any further, I think – to appease the traditionalistas and the trendophiles – we should be using the *Oxford English Dictionary* to define the word 'Vintage'. Just so we are all clear. OK?

VINTAGE *NOUN*

1. The year or place in which wine, especially wine of high quality, was produced.
2. Time that something of quality was produced.

VINTAGE *ADJECTIVE*

1. Relating to or denoting wine of high quality ('That's my vintage cabernet you are drinking – don't f**king spill it').
2. Denoting something from the past of high quality, especially something representing the best of its kind.

The etymology of the word vintage derives from the Latin *vindemia* (from *vinum* 'wine' + *demere* 'remove'). Remember that the next time you are asking for a vintage pair of socks, or whatever in a charity/thrift store.

BLACK AND WHITE

'I don't like anything that starts with 're' – like retro, reinvent, recreate – I hate that. It's always like living in the past – copying, emulating.'

Jack White, American musician and singer-songwriter

THE HISTORY OF BUNTING

Festivals, fetes, garage sales, street parties and church hall gatherings would be even duller events without the assistance of everybody's favourite type of festive decoration – bunting. But what is bunting, I hear you ask … and where the hell did it come from?

Bunting was first manufactured at the beginning of the 17th century – and was originally made from a lightweight fabric such as worsted wool. The British Royal Navy used it as signal flags, by using different colors and shapes, to alert or inform other passing ships using the International Code of Signals.

These days, bunting is a festive decoration. A series of decorated triangular flags strung together to make an area, or venue, look more pleasing (i.e. a gray office or a row of grimy terraced houses). In the USA bunting often bears the red, white and blue of the Stars and Stripes. In the UK, bunting is often in the same red, white and blue that comprises the Union Jack. In fact, most bunting is red, white and blue. However, if you ever see a colour combination that goes – RED – WHITE – GREEN – YELLOW – BLUE – RED – BLUE – WHITE then that is the International Code of Signals warning people to 'keep away', as there is a bunting-related event happening nearby.

VINTAGE VINTAGE

All this talk of vintage has, quite rightly, made me thirsty. And so it should. The word 'vintage' should only really be used to describe wine. Etymological pedantry aside however, I can report that the most expensive – and therefore proper vintage – bottle of white wine ever sold was a 1811 Château d'Yquem for the wallet-deflating cost of $117,000 (£75,000).

According to Guinness World Records this rare vintage was sold by the Antique Wine Company to French wine connoisseur, Christian Vanneque, in 2011.

To celebrate, I imagine Mr Vanneque probably had a big glass of wine.

Though probably not of his 1811 Château d'Yquem.

COZY DEATH

Actual scientists have worked out that the chances of death by a knitted tea cozy are 1 in 20 billion. But as it is possible to be injured by a tea cozy (see page 47), it could happen …

To put this ridiculous figure in to some sort of context, you (yes you!) have a 1 in 257,000 chance of dying today.

BIZARRE BAZAAR

In recent years, all over the developed world, flea markets, consignment shops, farmers' markets, garage sales, jumble sales, car boot sales, trash and treasure markets and swap shops have boomed, in part due to the global economic meltdown, but also for the amazing opportunities they present for acquiring rare, or antique items for next to nothing from people who have no idea what they are selling. These flea markets sell all manner of second-hand goods, from vintage clothing to retro knick-knacks. The US Flea Market is a veritable feast of the bazaar (and bizarre) …

* The USA has over 1,100 organized flea markets, as reported by the National Flea Market Association, and is worth $30 billion in annual sales to the economy.
* In the USA alone, over 150 million people visit flea markets each year.
* No fleas are actually sold – though many, we can presume, live on the vintage bomber jackets that are sold there.

MUST-'TACHE

'A man without a moustache is like a cup of tea without sugar.'

English proverb

JOLLY JUBILEE #1

In the week running up to Queen Elizabeth II's Diamond Jubilee in 2012, UK high street DIY retailer B&Q reported it had sold:

* 330,000ft (100,000m) of Union Jack bunting – that's one-tenth of the way to the Moon!
* 10,500 Jubilee cushions (sadly not whoopee).
* 3,100 Jubilee gnomes (sadly not of the Royal Family).

In the week after the Queen's Jubilee, landfills all over the UK suddenly became filled with:

* 330,000ft (100,000m) of Union Jack bunting.
* 10,500 Jubilee cushions.
* 3,100 Jubilee gnomes.

RETRO-ESQUE #1

'In the souls of the people the grapes of wrath are filling and growing heavy, growing heavy for the vintage.'

John Steinbeck, American author

VINTAGE BABY NAMES

There are some names that just sound old-fashioned. Malcolm is a pretty old-fashioned name. So is Mildred. You don't see many Malcolms and Mildreds on the dance floors of illegal raves these days, no matter where you live.

So it comes as no surprise that certain baby names are being considered 'vintage' – names that fill us with nostalgia of the 'good old glory days' when everybody was fighting a war or fighting off Polio.

Here are ten so-called vintage names that are making a comeback in 2013, according to US website babble.com.

1. Ada
2. Cora (popular again thanks to Countess Grantham in the vintage-soaked TV show *Downton Abbey*.)
3. Florence
4. Josie
5. Millie
6. Graham
7. Murray
8. Neville
9. Phinnaeus
10. Walter

HOW TO MAKE AN
AMERICAN QUILT

According to the Craft Yarn Council of America, 53 million American women (or 36 per cent of the total population) know how to knit or crochet, a 51 per cent increase since 1995.

THE VINTAGE MOVEMENT: AN ESSAY

In the 1980s there was a massive cultural shift in fashion. Modern designer labels were 'in' (i.e. trendy), *haute couture* was hot sh*t and anything that looked old was immediately put in the bin or up in the attic. When the vintage movement took off (again?) in the early noughties, everybody went back up into the attic (or kicked themselves for having thrown stuff away) and dug up all the stuff that now, all of a sudden, was cool again. Materials such as denim, fur, cords and leather (fabrics that are built to last a long time) were back in vogue.

The vintage movement that we are currently surviving is actually, I think, a backlash against the mass-produced, disposable fashion of high street clothing stores, where clothes are cheap, mass-marketed and affordable. The only downside is everybody is wearing the same clothes and everybody looks identical. With the Vintage Movement, because the source of the clothing varies from swap shops, charity stores, eBay etc., everybody feels like they are wearing something unique and something that has lasted and will continue to do so.

Clothing (and accessories) produced by high street chains doesn't last very long. Garments tend to last a season and then fall apart (or become 'so last season') – and while that's not the fault of the people employed to make them in ramshackle buildings for pitful wages, it is because of the flimsy fabrics they use.

And when these clothes fall apart, or start looking ratty, people give them away to charity shops. So where charity shops were once filled with quality vintage clothing (made of leather and long-lasting materials), now they are full to the brim with cheap, mass-produced clothes made from cheap fabrics.

So, the question is therefore, in 20 years time can vintage still exist? And can we call it vintage? The problem with the Vintage Movement of the moment is that consumers want the vintage *look* (at an affordable price) but they don't want the vintage clothing, which is expensive, and smells like it did originally in the 1970s.

VINGOOGLE-ESQUE

Guess how many search results come back if you type the word 'vintage' into Google – the modern day criteria for how popular something or someone really is. Go on, have a guess. It's ridiculous!

The answer is … 1,260,000,000 results.*

* Accurate at time of printing. It's probably tripled by now.

VINTAGE AROUND THE WORLD

Vintage junk is everywhere, no matter where you are or how hard you are trying to hide from it. But if you are planning on going traveling around Europe, watch out for the following translations of 'vintage' – it'll be those damn, sneaky foreigners trying to sell you something that looks old and smells funky and costs an arm and a leg.

Millésime – French
Epoca – Italian
Vendimia – Spanish
Berba grožđa – Croatian
Wijnoogst – Dutch
Ročník – Czech
Κρασι– Greek
Марочный – Russian
Rocznik wina – Polish

CORKER AU VIN

The world's oldest bottle of wine (proper vintage!) is reported to be a 1,650-year-old bottle of white wine, which was buried alongside its creator – a Roman noble living near Speyer, Germany – and sealed with wax. I say white wine – for all we know it could be just a bottle of the noble's urine or just really, really, old water.

Wine historians (people who have found an ingenious way to combine work and pleasure) believe the 'wine' was made in 350AD, then buried, only to be discovered in 1867, wherein it was analyzed by Kaiser Wilhelm II's chemists during the First World War. The bottle has been on display at the Pfalz Historical Museum in Germany for more than a century and, if opened, would definitely taste nothing like Mr Vanneque's 1811 Château d'Yquem (see page 8).

VINTAGE STAT #1

The average lifetime of a piece of clothing in the USA is only three years.

CRAFT GOES BOOM #1

Etsy, the Internet's largest online marketplace for crafting and a place where they like to 'keep it real' (their words not mine) now has over 7.5 million members. According to a 2012 report in *The Guardian*, Etsy has seen its total sales *double* in the UK since 2007.

RETRO-ISMS #1

In a modern context the word 'vintage' is often employed seriously as a word to mean, well, whatever you feel is appropriate and 'bang on-trend'. However, in reality (where I live), vintage is actually a euphemism often employed so vendors can add extra money onto the price tag. Something 'vintage' sounds expensive. Something 'flea-infested' does not.

Here's what we really mean when we say something is 'vintage' – and this is not just me being mean, these are actual words I found as I was nosing through the dictionary … and believe me, this is only the beginning!

Aged
Ancient
Antediluvian
Antiquated
Antique
Archaic
Battered
Beat-up
Clapped-out
Classic

RETRO-ESQUE #2

'I definitely spend the most money on shoes, partly because vintage footwear can be a little funky – in a bad way. I like to keep things pretty simple up top and then go weird with the shoes.'

Chloë Sevigny, American actress and fashion designer

REASONS BEHIND
THE VINTAGE TREND

You don't have to be a brain surgeon to work out why the global vintage trend has boomed over the years. In fact, you don't even need to be Paris Hilton to know why, but it is interesting to understand why this trend has truly taken off.

Here's why:

1. **The Global Economy** – thoughts, memories and objects of simpler times, of yesteryear, provide comfort in these harsh, cranky days of global economic meltdown.
2. **Staying in, austere times** – means more entertaining at home and making and fixing things for ourselves.
3. **Sod the High Street** – a backlash against mass-marketed, cheap fabric and disposable clothing that lasts as long as it takes to get out of the shop.
4. **Fashion cycles** – everything is cyclical. Cheap, mass-marketed clothes will be back. And we'll be calling them vintage, no doubt.

BETSY ROSS

Born in Philadelphia in 1752, Betsy Ross is commonly (if falsely) associated with sewing the first American flag. Though severely contested, the story goes that Betsy Ross 'made with her hands the first flag' of the USA.

The truth, from what I can make out, is that there were many flag makers at the time in Philadelphia, who would have also handmade the flag. However, there is evidence to suggest that Betsy's contribution to the design of the flag was to change the six-pointed stars to the five-pointed stars we see today. Apparently they were easier to sew.

BETSY-F**KING-ROSS

'I'm a seamstress? That's great. I come out of cryo-prison and I'm Betsy-f**king-Ross ...'

Sylvester Stallone, *Demolition Man*

UPCYCLING

Even recycling has been recycled into 2013's new favorite buzzword: upcycling.

Upcycling is an even greener way of recycling your old junk. You basically find a new purpose for your unwanted items before you chuck them away.

Here's my quick guide to upcycling.

BEFORE UPCYCLING	AFTER UPCYCLING
A lamp	A light
Wooden chair	A small table
A bedside cabinet	A deskside cabinet
Chest of drawers	A narrow table
Engagement ring	Napkin ring
Wedding dress	Table cloth
Teapot	Vase
Vase	Teapot
Cake stand	Hat stand
Tea cozy	Hat
Doily	Fancy bib

SEW WHAT #1

'Many estates are spent in the getting, since women for tea forsake spinning and knitting, and men for punch forsake hewing and splitting.'

Benjamin Franklin , American Founding Father

THE AGE OF
WONDERFUL NONSENSE

With the release of Baz Luhrmann's *The Great Gatsby*, the mainstream revival of period-style dancing on television on shows like *Dancing With the Stars*, as well as the international success of *Downton Abbey*, America is enjoying a 1920s love affair. Again.

Known as the Roaring Twenties, or the Age of Intolerance or the Jazz Age, 1920s America was actually a pretty turbulent and confused place with a mish-mash of emotions and movements. It was the decade that saw America turn into Modern America (the place we know now). The 1920s was a decade of self-indulgence, materialism, and frivolity and basically just a ten-year-long jolly after the ghastly realities of the Great War had sunk in. However, this modern idea of how wonderful this vintage decade was is slightly skewed by what it was actually like – the people who survived it were called the Lost Generation, after all. So, what do you think, were the 1920s really that great?

BAD THINGS	GOOD THINGS
The 18th Amendment: prohibition	The 19th Amendment: women given the right to vote
Only 35 per cent of homes with electricity	The first assembly line automobile
The Wall Street Crash	*The Great Gatsby*
Red Scares: fear of Communism	Baseball's Babe Ruth
Foreign policy isolationism	First motion picture, *The Jazz Singer*
The Great Depression	Charlie Chaplin
The rise of the Ku Klux Klan	The Charleston dance craze
Organized crime	Harry Houdini

BUNTINGOLOGY

Considering bunting is just a bunch of stupid triangles tied together with string, you'll be amazed, astounded and probably utterly dumbstruck to find out that 14,800,000 results are dumped onto your laptop when you Google it.

Though, obviously, a lot of that presumably has to do with baseball bunting …

BASEBALL BUNTING

Bunting in baseball is, according to the very entertaining *Baseball for Dummies*, when 'a batter holds the bat in the hitting zone and, without swinging, lets the ball make contact with it. The idea is to deaden the ball so that the base runners can advance (or the hitter can get to first base) while the opposing fielders run in to make a play.'

Bunting in baseball is a technical skill so therefore it's a billion times more interesting than those stupid decorative triangles people hang up …

KNIT YOUR OWN WEDDING

Exploiting the interest in all things royal since the wedding of Prince William and Kate Middleton in 2011, Fiona Gable's *Knit Your Own Royal Wedding Book has* sold a heart-attacking 45,000 copies to date.

Apparently, you need 19 miles (30.6km) of wool to knit Prince Charles' ears.

Ba-dum-tisch.

THE RISE OF
THE CHARITY SHOP

With the global economy in the gutter, there has been a less-than-surprising increase in UK shoppers (the squeezed middle classes) heading to their local charity shops hunting for bargains and, in the process, completely changing their shopping habits.

As a result, the UK charity shop business is feeling rather smug about itself, posting record profits and keeping Britain's high streets from knocking on death's gold-knockered door.

* Annual income in 2012 for UK charity shops reached an all-time high of almost £1 billion.
* The UK'S largest charity shop chain – The British Heart Foundation – generated a record-breaking profit of over £31 million between 2011 and 2012.

THE GROWTH OF BEARDS

Beards are back in fashion – yet more evidence of the influence of the retro and old-fashioned fashion brigade who are dictating what's hot and what's not. It seemed that beards belonged to a bygone era, but over the past few years, they have once again become socially acceptable. During the 1980s and 1990s, facial hair (apart from designer stubble *à la* George Michael) was a real social and fashion *faux pas*, a crime punishable by death. If you owned a beard, you were hiding something and were potentially a murderer. But now all that has been conveniently forgotten. Beards are hot again and 'on-trend'. That sounds ridiculous, doesn't it? It's just hair at the end of the day. But I don't make the rules.

However, beards are interesting from a sociological perspective. So, here are some furry facts to throw at any clean-cut, baby-faced wet-shavers who happen to be close by.

1. Dihydrotestosterone is the powerful male sex hormone that causes the body to mature during puberty but also promotes the growth of facial hair. It is up to ten times more powerful than regular ol' testosterone. Interestingly its power varies seasonally, which is why beards can be bushier in summer.

2. In Ancient civilizations beards were seen as a sign of honor – and they were only cut as a punishment.

3. Beards started to become unpopular (for the first time) around 345BC, when Alexander the Great decreed that soldiers could not have beards for fear of them being pulled on during battle. Makes sense.

4. Beard scientists believe single men shave more frequently than non-single men to make themselves seem less aggressive and more feminine. This makes women feel safer, apparently ('God knows what he's hiding underneath that beard!').

5. 98 per cent of *Forbes'* richest men are clean-shaven. 100 per cent of all known lumberjacks have beards. Probably.

RETRO-ESQUE #3

'Everything I buy is vintage and smells funny. Maybe that's why I don't have a boyfriend.'

Lucy Liu, American actress

PUNS THAT ARE
HANGING BY A THREAD

If you're intent on being a knit-wit, then these unseamly sewing puns are just for you.

Sewing is believing
Sew on and sew forth
Sew much fabric, sew little time
Because I say sew
You rip what you sew
Darn! My socks need mending
Funny puns like these have me in stitches (a hem)
And sew on and sew on ... you catch my drift

DON'T GET YOUR
KNITTERS IN A TWIST

No self-respecting book that involves knitting would be complete without a list of celebrities who have claimed – to the whole wide world – that they love knitting. Here are a few of the big-hitters of the A-list knitting community.

– Nicholas Hoult (actor)
– Ryan Gosling (actor)
– Jo Brand (comedian)
– Scarlett Johansson (actress)
– Katie Holmes (actress)
– Uma Thurman (actress)
– Kate Moss (fashion model)
– Hilary Swank (actress)
– Cameron Diaz (actress)
– Catherine Zeta-Jones (actress)
– Sarah Jessica Parker (actress)
– Winona Ryder (actress)
– Lily Allen (singer-songwriter)
– Madonna (singer-songwriter, director)
– Julia Roberts (actress)

VINTAGE STAT #2

One in four American women own seven pairs of jeans, but only wear four of them regularly.

Interestingly, one in four Americans also don't know what nation the USA declared independence from.*

* It was the British. *You knew that right?*

WHAT IS THE MEANING OF ALL THIS?

'Retro', 'vintage' and 'old-fashioned' are words that are bandied about these days with very little care. But they mean different things. Especially if you are trying to buy something. In the UK, if you're trying to sell an item as vintage when it's only ten years old, then you could get into some hot water with the Trade Descriptions Act of 1968. So, if you're going to sell any of your stuff on eBay or Craigslist, make sure you know the meaning of the lingo – otherwise you could get done for fraudulent advertising. And we wouldn't want that now, would we?

Merriam Webster describes 'retro' thusly:

RETRO *ADJECTIVE*

Relating to, reviving, or being the styles and especially the fashions of the past: fashionably nostalgic or old-fashioned.

STUPID THINGS PEOPLE SAY

One man's trash is another man's treasure.

(*The* Vintage motto, surely?)

DAYTIME TV

Daytime TV in the UK and USA is the stuff that nightmares are made of. And, coincidentally, most of the shows aired are about ordinary people finding 'vintage' and 'antique' junk in their attics and trying to sell them at auctions to other idiots who obviously don't have jobs to go to.

Here are ten of the very worst vintage-related daytime TV programs from both sides of the pond.

1. *Cash in the Attic* (BBC)
2. *Antiques Roadshow* (BBC and PBS)
3. *Bargain Hunt* (BBC)
4. *Flog It!* (BBC)
5. *Picked Off* (History Channel)
6. *American Pickers* (History Channel)
7. *Auction Hunters* (Spike TV)
8. *It's Worth What?* (NBC)
9. *Auctioneer$* (TLC)
10. *Pawn Stars* (History Channel)

INSTAGRAM

Launched in 2010, Instagram is now one of the world's most popular free photo sharing apps for smartphones. Basically, it allows you to put different filters onto your photos so it looks like they were taken by someone better than yourself – though sadly it doesn't remove fingers and thumbs from the lens. Some of Instagram's famous filters enhance the colors of the image and some dull them for effect but – and this has pleased many a pretentious hipster around the globe – most of the filters really just add a 1970s vintage feel to your photos. And it's this effect for which Instagram has really become worth more than its value.

* Instagram now has 100 million active monthly users.
* 40 million photos are uploaded every day!
* More than 1 billion Instagram photos have been uploaded so far.
* Instagram gains one new user every second.
* Facebook acquired Instagram in 2012 and valued it at $100,000,000.
* The Earlybird filter (the vintage one) is the second most popular filter out of the 17 available – 10 per cent of all photos uploaded use this.

SEW WHAT #2

'Women derive a pleasure, incomprehensible to the other sex, from the delicate toil of the needle.'

Nathaniel Hawthorne, *The Scarlet Letter*

COZY NIGHT IN ...
AT THE HOSPITAL

According to the UK's Department of Trade and Industry report on domestic accidents, 37 British people were admitted to the hospital for knitted tea cozy injuries in 1997 – up from 20 reported in 1996. That's not the tea cozy's fault, I know, but still ... knitting is dangerous.

CATH F**KING KIDSTON

Cath Kidston is now a household name and enemy number one in the fight against vintage. Whether you love or loathe her passion for all things retro, her floral-motif-based business empire is currently *everywhere* and she cannot be stopped. Cath Kidston stores are spreading around the world like the Norovirus and one day will be on every street corner of every city – like Starbucks.

99 per cent of the entire vintage you see these days has her name emblazoned in pastel on it.

The better you know you're enemy the safer you are, so the saying goes, so here are some facts about Cath Kidston you had better memorize – just in case she becomes the next Evil Overlord.

1. Cath Kidston set up her first store, or 'glorified junk shop' as she called it, in Holland Park, London, in 1993. Cath invested £15,000 of her own savings.
2. In 2013, Cath's shops were valued at over £75 million. She owns a 30 per cent stake in the business, reportedly worth £25 million. In 2009, profits rose by more than 60 per cent!
3. Cath Kidston employs over 650 staff in 28 stores in the UK, two in Ireland and seven in Japan; her website ships to the USA and Europe.
4. Cath has published three successful books – *Make*, *Sew* and *Stitch*.
5. In 2008, Ms Kidston designed bags for UK supermarket brand Tesco, made from recyclable plastic bags that would have ended up on landfill sites.

RETRO-ESQUE #4

'Old Americana vintage gangster stuff has a fantastical feel; it feels less dirty in a way. It feels like the opera of crime.'

Shia LaBeouf, American actor

AN OLDIE BUT A 'GOODIE'

Here is a selection of popular 'vintage songs' you are most likely to walk *away* from the dance floor to at the next wedding you attend. They may be 'classics' (there's that word again) but no one actually wants to listen to them.

The following songs or 'standards' (as the Vintage Police would call them) have been declared proper vintage by the Vintage Singer on his/her website, yep you guessed it, www.vintagesinger.com.

'Time After Time' – Frank Sinatra
'You Make Me Feel So Young' – Frank Sinatra
'Let There Be Love' – Nat King Cole
'Blue Moon' – Billie Holliday
'Cheek to Cheek' – Fred Astaire
'When I Fall in Love' – Doris Day
'Moon River' – Audrey Hepburn
'We'll Meet Again' – Vera Lynn
'Fly Me to the Moon' – Frank Sinatra
'As Time Goes By' – Engelbert Humperdinck
'Why Do Fools Fall in Love?' – Frankie Lymon
    & The Teenagers
'I've Got You Under My Skin' – Frank Sinatra
'It Had to Be You' – Ella Fitzgerald

ANTIQUE vs VINTAGE

Nowadays, 'vintage' is generally used as a euphemism for 'old', 'old-fashioned' or 'second-hand'.

In antiquing, however, an item is considered 'vintage' if it was manufactured between 1830 and 1930. In car collecting, for example, a vintage car is one made between 1919 and 1930.

THAT DRESS

Kate Middleton's wedding dress was one of the most talked about things of 2012. In fact it was talked about so much you could see all the hot air produced from space.

Costing a heart-stopping $416,700 (£250,000) the dress was anything but austere – but it was bang on-trend – with its vintage touches and classic style.

The dress was designed by Sarah Burton of über-trendy fashion house Alexander McQueen, and was an ivory gown with lace appliqué floral detail. The train was nearly 9ft (2.7m) long – which is roughly half the length of an average female great white shark.

THE EVOLUTION
OF THE FLAPPER

FLAPPER *NOUN*

A young fashionable woman intent on enjoying herself and flouting conventional standards of behavior (1920s).

SLAPPER *NOUN*

A young fashionable woman intent on enjoying herself and flouting conventional standards of behavior (2000s).

DECOUPAGE #1

What is decoupage?

It's where French farmers keep their chickens.*

* It's not really (see page 59).

CRAFTY NATION

Figures released in 2011 report that the Craft and Hobby industry in the USA is worth $29 billion, with around 56 per cent of households crafting at least once a year.

A survey of 114,200,000 US households produced the following results, which show how the craft industry is accounted for. Interesting stuff, if your definition of the word 'interesting' is completely different to mine.

Top Ten Craft Segments by Sales

Woodworking and wood crafts	$3.322 billion
Drawing	$2.078 billion
Food crafting	$2.001 billion
Jewelry making	$1.446 billion
Scrapbooking and memory crafts	$1.440 billion
Floral decorating	$1.303 billion
Crocheting	$1.062 billion
Card making	$1.040 billion
Home décor crafts	$948 million
Wedding crafts	$803 million

Top Ten Craft Segments by Household Participation

Drawing	$21.1 million
Scrapbooking and memory crafts	$18.4 million
Crocheting	$17.4 million
Woodworking and wood crafts	$16.8 million
Jewelry making	$14.7 million
Card making	$14.0 million
Floral decorating	$13.6 million
Cross-stitch	$13.3 million
Knitting	$13.0 million
Wreath making	$11.6 million

BUZZ OFF

BBC TV has followed hot on the heels of the success of *The Great British Bake Off* with the slightly more annoying *The Great British Sewing Bee*. In the same way GBBO (Yes, I'm abbreviating it – every time I write it out in full I waste ten seconds of my life) started a cake revolution, the GBSB is laser-focused on starting a sewing revolution.

With a mega 2.5 million people in the UK tuning in to the show's first episode, it would seem that world knitting domination is inevitable.

pokes both eyes out with knitting needles

DECOUPAGE #2

The old-fashioned art of decorating an object by glueing colored paper cutouts onto it, alongside other paint effects and trimmings such as gold leaf.*

Now that you know what it is, you can do your best to avoid it at all costs.

* Thanks Wikipedia.

DOWNTON DRESSES

The international success of ITV's *Downton Abbey* has sparked a furious frenzy over 1920s-era dresses and fashions. So much so that many fashion brands have seen an increase in 'retro flapper-style dresses and demure ruffled blouses' (the *Daily Mail*).

However it isn't just the dresses from the show that has got us all out of breath: the 1920s nightwear worn by the main female characters has also taken off.

Originally established in 1890, luxury British lingerie brand Lucile has reported an unprecedented increase in sales – due to a brief mention on the show. Lucile was an incredibly popular brand in the 1920s and is now enjoying a revival that has seen overall sales increase by 48 per cent since *Downton Abbey* aired its second series in the UK.

Lucile has been revived by Camilla Blois, the great great granddaughter of the brand's original creator, Lady Duff Gordon, and is in its first season of flaunting its wares.

ETSY BITSY TEENY WEENY YELLOW POLKA DOT BIKINI

Launched in the USA in 2005, Etsy has become the go-to website for handmade, vintage craft items and supplies. One of their guidelines is that all 'vintage' items must be more than 20 years old. They sell all manner of old-fashioned knick-knacks ranging from jewelry to quilts. Need to know more? OK then …

* Over 1.29 billion page views in the month of May 2012.
* It's the 56th most popular website in the USA, and the 170th most popular website in the world.
* 690,000 new members join every month.
* It's valued at $600 million and employees 263 staff.
* Etsy sales increased 71 per cent in the year 2010–2011.
* 2,900,000 items sold per month.
* The number one most pinned site on Pinterest.
* Etsy takes a 3.5 per cent cut of all sales.
* 50 per cent of all members are aged 18–34 (so not the Gray Market, as you might have expected).

VINTAGE COCKTAILS

Nostalgia-soaked TV shows such as *Mad Men* have got us all drunk on lust for Don Draper's devilish ways, as well as his love of vintage cocktails, vintage machismo and vintage smoking – so much so in fact that our lungs and livers are starting to seize up.

However, if *Mad Men* is not your cup of tea, and you see it as nothing more than a flimsy one-note concept exploiting our yearning for yesteryear, but you end up having to watch it anyway, then you may need a drink or five to get you through each monochrome-colored episode. If so, try one of the following vintage cocktails to give you some Dutch courage.

VINTAGE COCKTAILS #1
OLD FASHIONED

YOU WILL NEED
1 thick slice orange peel
1 maraschino cherry, with stem
1 tsp sugar syrup (also sold as gomme syrup)
2–3 drops whisky bitters
ice cubes, as necessary
2fl oz (60ml) scotch or bourbon
twist of lemon peel, to garnish

MIX IT UP
1. Take the orange peel and squeeze it with your fingers. Rub the peel around the inside of a whisky tumbler and then place into the glass. Add the cherry, sugar syrup and bitters, along with three ice cubes.
2. Add half of the scotch or bourbon and stir for about ten seconds. Add more ice and the remaining scotch or bourbon and stir again for 10–15 seconds. To serve, garnish with lemon peel.

RETRO-ESQUE #5

'I spent my first paycheck on a vintage Mercedes.'

Jennifer Aniston, American actress

RETRO COMPUTER GAMES

We could spend all day talking about what's considered retro and what's not. But I think it's fair to say that anything from the 1980s can now be called 'retro', and anything from the 1970s is regarded as 'hippy chic'.

There are, however, certain computer games (and consoles – like the Spectrum ZX or Omega), and many of the first ever websites, that are now definitely 'retro' – so much so that they are even collector's items, despite being only 20 years old.

How many of these 'classic' games did you play at the 'arcade' – the place which, ironically, you still go to all the time, but is now a Starbucks.

1. *Street Fighter*
2. *Pong*
3. *Tetris*
4. *Sonic the Hedgehog*
5. *Asteroids*
6. *Super Mario World*
7. *Space Invaders*
8. *Doom*
9. *Snake*
10. *Pac Man*

CRAFT GOES BOOM #2

Because of a thrilling report by the UK's Craft Council, some poor egghead had to calculate that there had been an eye-popping 500 per cent rise in sales of sewing machines during 2012 – 500 per cent! This is all thanks to the resurgence of crafting on popular TV programs (shown in primetime schedule slots) such as Kirstie Allsopp's *Homemade Britain* on Channel 4 and the BBC's *Great British Sewing Bee.*

VINTAGE JOKES #1

People often say that when it comes to jokes the 'old ones are the best' but often they're just joking when they say that – because it's not true. You don't believe me? Take a look at these vintage 'classics' …

Why did the chicken cross the road?
To get to the other side.

What do you get when you cross a dog with a telephone?
A Golden Receiver.

What did the dog say when he sat on the sandpaper?
Rough! Rough!

Why was the computer so tired when it got home?
Because it had a hard drive!

What do you call a chicken in a shell suit?
An egg.

VINTAGE STAT #3

Americans generate almost 13 million tons of textile waste per year. Brits generate about 1.12 million tons of textile waste each year.

DEAR BUNTERS

Dear bunting makers,
All bunting seems to be made using isosceles or equilateral triangles. Why not throw in a few right-angled or scalene triangles for variation, huh?

Don't be so square – mix things up a little.

GUERRILLA KNITTING

A new craze (*and it is crazy!*) is currently sweeping through the UK in 2013. The website 'Knit the City' describes 'yarnstorming' or 'yarnbombing' as 'the art of enhancing a public place or object with graffiti knitting'.

Sew basically, you run wild through the city streets and cover a telephone box, or statue, with a piece of knitting and then run away. Sounds 'fun'.

BEARDED NATION

33 per cent of the US male population has facial hair.

55 per cent of the worldwide population has facial hair (excluding hairy women).

RETRO-ISMS #2

More words that mean exactly the same as 'vintage' (but don't cost you your arms, legs or any other part of your body).

Decrepit
Dilapidated
Down-at-heel
Elderly
Flea-bitten
Historic
Mangy
Moth-eaten
Museum piece
Old-fashioned
Out-moded

WASTERS

In the wardrobes of UK consumers there are, according to a 2012 report, 1.7 billion items of clothing hanging up unused. This adds up to an embarrassing £30 billion worth of clothing that nobody wears.

I'm not just making these numbers up. These are figures reported by WRAP, the UK's leading body on resource efficiency. Here are some other pretty horrifying statistics.

* If you simply increase the 'active use' of your clothing by an extra nine months you could reduce the water, carbon and waste impacts by up to 20–30 per cent each and save the country £5 billion.
* One-third of all of the clothes we buy in the UK ends up in landfill.
* Used clothing has a massive commercial value, yet over 430,000 tons is thrown away in the UK every year.

SEW WHAT #3

'As I get older, I just prefer to knit.'

Tracey Ullman, English actress and comedian

IN FOR A PENNY

US thrift stores are now a multi-billion-dollar industry thanks to 'value-conscious consumers who have an increasing awareness of the importance of reducing pointless waste, we are progressing from a disposable society to a recycling society.'

A report by First Research estimates the resale industry in the USA has annual revenues of approximately $13 billion.

According to America's Research Group, 16–18 per cent of Americans will shop at a thrift store during a given year.

To put that figure into context:

* 11.4 per cent of Americans shop in factory outlet malls.
* 21.3 per cent of Americans shop in major department stores.
* Thrift store sales increased 12.7 per cent as the US economy worsened.
* Designer jeans cost, on average, $175 compared to department store jeans at an average of $52. Thrift store jeans cost just $8.

IMMENSE SATISFACTION

'I get immense satisfaction from wearing things I've had for years as I take good care of them or recycle them into something new.'

Kirstie Allsopp, British TV property and home expert (who describes herself on Twitter as 'A working Mum who's against homework & for family time; Re-use, recycle, love, laugh & Keep Britain Tidy!')

KNITTING UP

According to Google, in 2011, 'dressmaking' searches were around 100,000 in the UK, and sewing-related searches were hitting 600,000 a month. Knitting-related queries were reaching over a million a month.

If you add all that up, that's over 20 million a year!

ONE REASON TO NEVER, EVER BUY VINTAGE CLOTHES. EVER

BEDBUGS

Vintage clothes shopping at your local thrift store or charity shop may sound like a great way to grab bargains, but be warned, as it comes at the risk of taking home a lot more than you bargained for.

Taken from the scary but informative website www.bedbug.com – and because I'm a nice guy – here are the tips you need if you're stupid enough to buy clothes from people (whom you've never met) and who have already thrown those clothes away once before.

1. If you must buy that second-hand blouse, check it inside and out for signs of bed bugs. This is especially important for clothes with ruffles, creases, seams etc.

2. Is the store very cluttered with piles of clothing or clothes on the floor? These conditions provide extra spaces for bed bugs to hide, so be cautious and check your clothing before purchasing.
3. The cleaner the store, the less likely it is to have bed bugs.
4. If traveling home on public transportation, keep clothing bags elevated, preferably in your hand or on top of metal, which bed bugs cannot easily climb on.
5. Check the exterior and interior of clothing again before entering the house.
6. Wash newly purchased clothing as soon as you get it using high temperatures to ensure that any bed bugs that have been lying in wait cannot survive.
7. If you do discover you have bought clothing with bed bugs, wash it as above, and notify the store so they don't continue selling clothing that may have bed bugs.
8. Try not to put your stuff down on non-metal and un-elevated surfaces. If you see a pile of clothes that aren't yours, keep them separate from your own.

And there you go – your top tips for buying clothes other people didn't want and you have no idea where they might have been ...

THE CRAFT MARKET

Why are we experiencing this growth in all things homemade?

Selected from a list, the reasons for buying or considering buying craft for half or more of the sample are that: 'Craft makes a unique gift' (58 per cent); 'I admire the human skill involved/want to keep craft skills alive' (55 per cent) and 'Beautiful objects appeal to me' (49 per cent).

The reasons chosen by over a third of the sample are: 'It means I own something that nobody else does' (41 per cent); 'I like to have beautiful objects in my home' (39 per cent); and 'To support craft people/makers' (35 per cent).

RETRO-ESQUE #6

'Women can explore so much in dressing. But if I was a guy I would wear vintage suits constantly. With crazy ties!'

Helena Christensen, Danish fashion model and photographer

PINS AND NEEDLES

Knitting is getting out of hand in the UK with more people knitting now than when knitting was invented – even though we now have loads of cool machines and technology that do it for us. OK, that's a lie. But you believed me that it could be true – and that's what is worrying.

Next time you get on a bus you could be sitting next to a knitter. And, if you're in London, they'll probably be knitting at the time. Knitting on public transport has become the new trend in the UK. Worrying thought isn't it?

If you do sit next to a knitter on the bus, why not disarm them with these factoids; hopefully then they'll realize just how silly they look.

*   It is estimated there are between 4–7 million knitters in the UK.
*   448,000 men sew in the UK.
*   In 2012 there were over 462 knitting groups listed in the UK.

VINTAGE COCKTAILS #2
CLASSIC MARTINI

Oh look, *Downton Abbey*'s on, you may need another vintage cocktail to help you survive the night …

YOU WILL NEED
2½ fl oz (75ml) gin
2½ fl oz (75ml) dry vermouth
3 green olives

MIX IT UP
1. Rinse the martini glass with dry vermouth and pour out.
2. Shake gin with ice until chilled.
3. Pour into a martini glass, add the olives and serve.

LAND FULL

Americans throw away 1,000,000,000 (that's a billion) shopping bags, every year, creating 300,000 tons of landfill waste. Many of these bags are used to carry junk from thrift stores and then become junk themselves – with both items ending up as landfill waste together, usually within a year of first meeting.

VINTAGE ETSY

According to Etsy's policy, 'the Vintage category is for items that are at least 20 years old.'

Twenty years old – that's going back to 1983 – that's hardly vintage, is it? That's retro. When does antique kick in?

TEN THINGS THAT USED TO BE OLD BUT ARE NOW RETRO. I THINK

It's hard to keep up with what's retro and what's just plain old junk. Surely it depends on how old you are and how much you really care about such things. Where does 'retro' start and 'rubbish' begin? I'm no expert, but I think the items listed below used to be deemed crap – and outdated – but are now regarded as stylishly retro and 'old-school'. I could be wrong – but how many of them did you own?

1. Digital watch
2. 8mm camera
3. Calculator
4. Typewriter
5. Tape cassette player or boombox
6. Rotary dial telephone
7. 8-bit computer game cartridges
8. Pez dispenser
9. Polaroid camera
10. Sneakers

KNITTED GOSLING

Ryan Gosling – the world's most fanciable man* – is a self-proclaimed knitter. Well, sort of. He mentioned it once in an interview with *GQ Australia*. This is what he said:

'I did this scene in *Lars and the Real Girl* where I was in a room full of old ladies who were knitting, and it was an all-day scene, so they showed me how. It was one of the most relaxing days of my life! If I had to design my perfect day, that would be it. And you get something out of it at the end. You get a nice present. For someone who wants an oddly shaped, off-putting scarf.'

* Not my personal opinion. I'm more of a George Clooney kind-of-a-guy.

SEW WHAT #4

'The innocent sleep, Sleep that knits up the ravell'd sleave of care.'

William Shakespeare, English poet and playwright

VINTAGE ON FACEBOOK

Where the modern meets the old: on Facebook over 244,395 people like the concept of vintage. That's right, someone set up a Facebook page, labeled it 'Vintage', and 244,395 people 'liked' it. For no other reason than because it included the word 'vintage'.

PURLS OF WISDOM

Too much knitting can increase the chance of a self-induced fatal stabbing incident by up to 35 per cent*. Knitting can also be a major cause of repetitive strain injury (RSI), which affects hundreds of thousands of workers in the USA and costs more than $20 billion in workers' compensation, so to all you knit-wits out there, be careful …

* OK, I made this one up.

RETRO-ESQUE #7

'There's a vintage which comes with age and experience.'

Jon Bon Jovi, American musician and actor

VINTAGE INSULTS

Calling people you don't like names that make you laugh is one of the simplest (and best) remaining joys of modern life (well, when your beer money has run out).

Why not pick up your modern iPhone now and call someone one of the following old-fashioned words that have sadly fallen out of step with the new-age world, and are never likely to be called back into action. Trust me, they'll have no idea what you're talking about …

1. **Snollygoster** – someone who is guided by personal advantage rather than by principles. Example: Dick Cheney.
2. **Slubberdeguillon** – someone with no worth, a moron. Example: George W. Bush.
3. **Gomorgan** – an evil monster. Examples: Kim Jong-un, Dick Cheney.
4. **Flibbertigibbet** – a ridiculous person, a gossip. Example: Perez Hilton.

CHARITY BEGINS ON THE HIGH STREET

There are now more than 5,500 charity shops in the UK. This exponential rise in charity shops has been aided by important tax breaks. These breaks ensure that all charity chains pay only 20 per cent of standard business rates. I have no idea what that means – but it sounds like a step in the right direction.

VINTAGE JOKES #2

What does Doctor Who eat with his pizza?
Dalek bread.

How do you turn a duck into a soul singer?
Put in a microwave until its Bill Withers.

What do you call a man with a seagull on his head?
Cliff.

What do you call a deer with no eyes?
No idea.

SEW FUNNY #1

'I got a sewing machine for my husband.
Good trade, huh?'

BACK TO THE FUTURE

The *Back to the Future* movie trilogy kickstarted – or at least aided on a mainstream level – popular culture's love affair a) with itself and b) its past.

In the movies, our anti-hero Marty McFly travels back in time from the harsh, unpleasant present of 1985 (when the film was made), to the simple, joyous year of 1955, where everything from the girls' dresses, classic cars, diners, technology and even parental relationships, were all played as vintage parodies of what an 1980s audience thought the 1950s had been like. In the second movie, Marty travels to the future, to the year 2015 and then back to 1955. In the final movie, Marty travels to 1885, becomes a cowboy and from that point on I get a bit confused. Anyway, here are my favorite time-related quotes for you to enjoy.

Dr. Emmett Brown: 'If my calculations are correct, when this baby hits 88 miles per hour … you're gonna see some serious s**t.'

Marty McFly: 'Whoa. This is heavy.'

Dr. Emmett Brown: 'There's that word again. "Heavy." Why are things so heavy in the future? Is there a problem with the Earth's gravitational pull?'

Dr. Emmett Brown: 'I'm sure that in 1985, plutonium is available in every corner drugstore, but in 1955, it's a little hard to come by.'

Marty McFly: [watching a *Honeymooners* episode in 1955] 'Hey, hey, I've seen this one. I've seen this one. This is a classic. This is, uh, where Ralph dresses up as a man from space.'

Milton Baines: 'What do you mean, you've seen this? It's brand new.'

Marty McFly: 'Yeah, well, I saw it on a … rerun.'

Milton Baines: 'What's a rerun?'

Marty McFly: 'You'll find out.'

Lorraine Baines: 'Well, you're safe and sound now, back in good old 1955.'

VINTAGE DAY

Every year in the UK that bastion of tradition, the National Trust, holds a Vintage Day where you can 'spend a leisurely day celebrating all things vintage: clothes, jewelry, accessories and a pop-up hair stylist will be on site. Come and enjoy your favorite hits from the 1940s, 1950s, 1960s, and 1970s. Play games and dress up in classic clothing from a bygone era. For children there will be cupcake decorating and eating.'

Children get to have all the fun.

CHARITY ENDS ON
THE HIGH STREET

According to the Charity Shops Survey of 2012, sponsored by the Charity Retail Association (a real page-turner I'm sure), here are the top ten charity shops in the UK.

CHARITY	NO. SHOPS	PROFIT PER SHOP PER WEEK
1. British Heart Foundation	709	£869
2. Oxfam	685	£811
3. Cancer Research	554	£712
4. Age UK	451	£374
5. Barnardo's (children)	487	£406
6. Sue Ryder (health and social care)	392	£396
7. British Red Cross	318	£372
8. Scope (disability)	237	£228
9. Salvation Army	135	£1,725
10. PDSA (pets)	179	£259

THE NOT-SO-GREAT GATSBY

The first edition of *The Great Gatsby* by F. Scott Fitzgerald – the on-trend, of-the-moment vintage book/film – was published in the USA in April 1925. It is now regarded as a masterpiece and one of the greatest American novels of the 20th century.

* Charles Scribner and Sons, the publisher, printed only 20,870 copies of the first edition.
* F. Scott Fitzgerald was paid an author's advance of $2,000 in 1921 to write the book. That's $21,233 in today's money. Another payment of $16,666 was paid to the author for the film rights in 1926.
* A copy of the first edition hardback of *Gatsby* sold for a record $182,000 in 2009 at Bonham's rare book auction in New York.

KNITSTATS

According to a report in 2011 on the Craft industry in the USA, it was claimed that, on average, every American (including men, women and children) spent $910 on more than 62 garments in 2011.

OLD-FASHIONED IDIOMS

If you are an idiot (what I call someone who uses idioms) then you have probably used a few of these pointless vintage-related phrases recently. Try not to in the future though – we're trying to embrace the future remember?

1. A bird in the hand is worth two in the bush
2. A dime a dozen
3. A fool and his money are soon parted
4. A penny saved is a penny earned
5. An arm and a leg
6. Everything but the kitchen sink
7. From rags to riches
8. Get down to brass tacks
9. Haste makes waste
10. Hell in a handbasket
11. Let bygones be bygones
12. Never bite the hand that feeds you
13. Pass the buck
14. You can't judge a book by its cover
15. You can't take it with you
17. Old hat
18. Needle in a haystack

LAND FULL AGAIN

Despite us certainly recycling more than we ever have, the UK still buries 50 per cent of its waste in the ground. One day in many years to come, future humans will look at the retro and vintage junk we are throwing away now and think that we *really* must have been living in the past.

The UK throws away so much waste every year (almost 30 million tons) that it would fill 3.5 million double-decker buses – a queue of which would stretch from London to Sydney (Australia) and back! And bus passes aren't cheap either. Or recyclable.

VINTAGE CARS

Vintage cars, classic cars, collector cars, whatever you want to call them – all you need to know is that they are ridiculously expensive. Ladies and gentlemen, I give you just ten of the most expensive *vintage* cars in the world.

1. 1963 Ferrari 250 GTO $32 million, 2012.
2. Vadim's 1959 Ferrari 250 GTO LWB $5.8 million, 2012.
3. 1957 Ferrari 625 TRC Spider $6.5 million, 2012.
4. 1991 Aston Martin DB4GT Zagato Sanction II Coupé $1.9 million, 2012.
5. Bugatti 57SC Atlantic coupe $30-40 million, 2010.
6. 1957 Ferrari 250 Testa Rossa $12.2 million, 2009.
7. 1959 Ferrari 250 GT LWB California Spider Competizione $7.2 million, 2009.
8. 1933 Alfa Romeo 8C 2300 Monza $6.7 million, 2010.
9. 1961 Ferrari 250 GT SWB Berlinetta SEFAC Hot Rod $6.11 million, 2010.
10. 1957 Ferrari 250 Testa Rossa fully restored $16.39 million, 2011.

RETRO-ESQUE #8

'It is easily overlooked that what is now called vintage was once brand new.'

Tony Visconti, American record producer

RETRO-ISMS #3

Let's be honest, people say 'vintage' but what they really mean is … (this is it, I promise).

Period
Rare
Ratty
Relic
Rickety
Shabby
Tatty
Throwback
Time-tested
Time-worn
Traditional
Venerable

iKnit 2.0

In 2011, Google Analytics UK showed the search term 'knitting for beginners' had increased by 250 per cent.

VINTAGE COCKTAILS #3
WARHOL MANHATTAN

Surely, you must be drunk by now? No? Try this …

YOU WILL NEED

1½ fl oz (45ml) Martini Rosso vermouth

1½ fl oz (45ml) Dewar's White Label blended scotch whisky

3 cherries soaked in premium orange liqueur

MIX IT UP

1. Shake the liquid ingredients with ice.
2. Strain into a martini cocktail glass or pour over ice in a tumbler.
3. Drop in the cherries and serve.

VINTAGE JOKES #3

Why did the cow cross the road?
To get to the udder side.

Where did Napoleon keep his armies?
Up his sleevies.

What's green and hairy and goes up and down?
A gooseberry in a lift.

Two budgies standing on a perch.
One says, 'Can you smell fish?'

RETRO-ESQUE #9

'I would never wear fur, although I guess if it was a really vintage piece you might just get away with it.'

Kelly Osbourne, British TV presenter

VINYL POWER

Along with cars, bikes, clothing, furniture – basically anything you can think of that you can sell – the lust for all things vintage and retro has also influenced the vinyl record market. The UK's Entertainment Retailers Association (ERA) reported in January 2013 that the value of the vinyl album market had increased by nearly 70 per cent in 2012, with a total of 389,000 vinyl records sold according to figures from the Official Charts Company and the BPI.

The world's oldest – and therefore most antique – record shop, Spillers in Cardiff, Wales, has sold vinyl records since 1894.

VINTAGE STAT #4

The US textile recycling industry creates around 17,000 jobs and saves 2.5 billion pounds (1.13 billion kilos) of post-consumer textile product from going to waste each year.

SEW FUNNY #2

Quilters never cut corners.

CAT'S MEOW

In the 1920s, women were given the right to vote in national elections. One giant leap forward, for sure. However, that didn't put an end to male chauvinism (a very popular pastime back then), with a vast array of ridiculously un-PC words spouting out of many a manly mouth.

In fact, period 1920s slang was pretty stupid too. And – surprise, surprise – these throwback terms are making a comeback. How many of the following have you heard recently?

Bearcat – a hot and fiery lady.
Mind your beeswax – mind your own business.
Baloney – nonsense.
Cat's meow – something stylish.
Dame – a female.
Flapper – a hedonistic woman.
Gams – a woman's legs.
Heebie-jeebies – nerves.
Hooch – alcohol.
Joint – a bar.
Spiffy – an elegant appearance/a vintage appearance.
Swell – wonderful.

MORE MONEY THAN SENSE

According to vintage website etsy.com, one of the most ridiculous items that has been sold was a piece of meteorite that looks like a monk screaming. It went for $91,199.99.

A bedazzled chair went for $21,000.

VINTAGE SMOKER

Many of the popular period TV shows of the moment, such as *Mad Men* and *Downton Abbey*, have made smoking look cool again. Which, as we all now know, is dangerous to our health. Here are some very un-reassuring statistics about smoking.

Interestingly, today only 19.8 per cent of Americans smoke, compared to 1950 when it was estimated that half the population smoked. The Office of Smoking Statistics reports that 369.8 billion cigarettes were smoked in 1950 and 360 billion were smoked last year. Given the population of the USA is more than double what it was in 1950 that demonstrates the fall in the number of smokers (or the number of cigarettes they are actually smoking).

In 1950, smoking was permitted in public places; as of July 2009, 24 states prohibit smoking in most public places.

The 1920s were the decade where Americans 'blew off steam' after the end of the Great War. Literally, it seems. In 1924, 73 billion cigarettes were sold in the USA, and the population was only 105 million! That works out as 695 cigarettes each per year for every man, woman and child.

STUPID-STITIONS

Ever get the feeling you've been lied to? Well, this vintage explosion has also got people dusting off once-popular superstitions and sayings and making them all trendy again.

Please don't believe any of this nonsense. Here are the worst old-fashioned sayings currently doing the rounds.

It's bad luck to let milk boil over (it's just careless).

Never tread on a grave (what are you doing in a graveyard anyway, weirdo?).

Never give a knife or scissors as a gift ('You shouldn't have. No seriously. You shouldn't have …').

Burning cheeks means someone is talking about you (more likely to be having a hot flush).

A sudden chill that causes a shiver means someone has stepped over your grave (even though you are alive when it happens?).

When a dog howls, death is near (or it's just hungry).

If you bite your tongue whilst eating it's because you've recently told a lie (or again are just careless).

A bride must sew a swan's feather into her husband's pillow to ensure fidelity (good luck getting a swan's feather, those creatures are vicious).

It's bad luck to open an umbrella indoors (it's also pointless – it doesn't rain inside).

RETRO-ESQUE #10

'I go to vintage stores rather than high-end boutiques, because I like to dress different from other people.'

Ashley Benson, American actress and fashion model

E PLURIBUS UNUM

'Old things are always in good repute, present things in disfavor.'

Publius Cornelius Tacitus, a senator and a historian of the Roman Empire

OLD FASHIONED WORDS
MAKING A COMEBACK

Even though the English language re-invents itself every year, and words dip in and out of fashion as quickly as those meerkats who pop their heads up out of the sand, there are some 'old-fashioned' words making a comeback in our recycling-savvy culture. How many of them have you used lately?

Ahoy – hello!
Brouhaha – an overexcited interest in an event.
Crikey – an expression of alarm or excitement.
Fisticuffs – a fight.
Flabbergasted – speechless.
Flummoxed – bewildered.
Gobbledegook – nonsense.
Harrumph – disapproval.
Nincompoop – a stupid person.
Plebs – common people.
Tarnation – a euphemism for damnation.
Wally – a friendly idiot.

THE UNBELIVABLE TRUTH

In 2011 in the UK, creative kitchenware and cookware solutions for the home and creative crafts company Lakeland reported sales of icing bags, piping equipment and muffin cases have increased by one third, while sales of vintage-style tins and stands more than doubled.

NEEDLE IN A HAYSTACK

On 10 March 2008, the largest knitting needles ever made were – wait for it – used to knit a tension square of ten stitches by ten rows at the Metro Radio Arena, Newcastle upon Tyne, UK.

The massive needles measured 11½ ft (3.5m) long with a diameter of 3⅕ in (8cm) and were made by knitting fanatic (presumably) Ingrid Wagner.

Still, if Ingrid ever lost them in a haystack at least she'd be able to find them.

VINTAGE STAT #5

Over 70 per cent of the world's population uses second-hand clothes.

VINTAGE ITEMS
MAKING A COMEBACK

From researching exhaustively on Etsy the following items are being brought back from the dead (and from the back of the closet) and are making a classic comeback in 2013.

* Lazy Susans – classic retro!
* Napkin rings
* Cigarette boxes
* Sugar bowls
* Bookends
* Doilies – modern antique!
* Copper tea kettles
* Milk jugs
* Cup cake stands – old-school vintage!
* Teapots
* Sweet bowls
* Thermos flasks – keeps tea warm!

How many of these items do you have? The correct answer should be zero.

GROSS CRAFT

The combined Gross Value Added of the craft industry in the UK (or put simply, how much more the raw materials of wool etc. are worth once they are finished jumpers etc.) is £220m.

RETRO-ESQUE #11

'My vintage T-shirt collection is a little ridiculous.'

Josh Henderson, American actor and fashion model

VINTAGE STAT #6

One in five Brits admits to throwing away a garment after a single wear. This means that more than $127 million of clothing is binned (and presumably ends up as landfill) each year after being worn just once.

JUST THE FACTS, MA'AM

A recent report by the UK's Craft Council to establish 'the current size, value and characteristics of the craft market in England' was released and threw up (as I did when reading it) the following 'vital' statistics.

The total market – buyers plus potential buyers – for craft is 26.5 million people (63 per cent of the adult population of England).

NATIONAL
KNITTING WEEK

It's that time of year again.*

National Knitting Week 2013 runs in the UK from 14–21 October.

* To leave the country.

JOLLY JUBILEE #2

In May 2012, the *Daily Mail* 'reported' (it's hardly news is it? IS IT?) that Union Jack cake stands sales had risen by a hair-raising 2,783 per cent.

This ridiculous bit of journalism also went on to announce that Union Jack teacups and saucers sales were up 5,588 per cent. Obviously, I have no idea how many teacups and saucers were sold beforehand, but when percentages are in the thousands instead of hundreds, then we should all worry.

RETRO-ESQUE #12

'All of a sudden, Hulk Hogan has become retro. Hulk Hogan has become cool again.'

Hulk Hogan, American wrestler, actor and reality TV star

FEELING DOWNTON?

It's official. The news is just in. Maybe you should pull up a chair?

In recent figures released by the Public Broadcasting System (PBS) which airs the show, *Downton Abbey* has broken all TV records in the USA with season three collecting an eye-popping 24 million viewers overall – the highest-rated TV drama in PBS's history. That's one-third of the UK in one sitting!

For the finale of season three, the show became the highest-rated program across the whole of American TV that particular Sunday evening and beat-off *all* broadcast and cable competition. For 60 minutes in the USA, *Downton Abbey* was the place to be.

That particular episode is the one where Matthew dies. Oh sorry, did you not know that? Hope I haven't spoiled it for you. Sorry, this sentence should have started with SPOILER ALERT!

ROSE-TINTED SPECTACLES

The British are a nation obsessed with our past. Whether we are nostalgic for our 'glory years' or hell-bent on preserving our history, the Brits are a country of retronauts venturing back to a past when everything was deemed rosy and glorious. Though is that strictly true? Were the bygone days of yesteryear as great as the nostalgia-addicts and vintage-freaks make out? Let's compare 1952 and 2013, shall we?

	1952	2013
Average working week	40–48hrs	37hrs
Annual holiday	16 days	28 days
Total population	50 million	62.3 million
Workforce	23 million	32 million
Cost of a pint of milk	4p	50p
Weekly wage	£7.50	£500
Pint of beer	9p	£2.80
House price	£2,000	£163,000
Percentage of people employed	96 (men) 46 (women)	75 (men) 66 (women)
Manufacturing jobs	8.7 million	2.5 million
Public sector jobs	6 million	6 million
No. private sector firms	160,000	4.5 million

And the winner is: 2013.

RETRO THRILLER

In 1983, Michael Jackson released the pop music video for his latest release, 'Thriller'. Both the song and its video were massive hits. In the video, MJ can be seen wearing a retro – and iconic – red and black jacket that started a trend which, at the time, was called the 'hottest outerwear fad of the 1980s' as it apparently epitomized 1980s teen cool.

The jacket is now considered iconic in its retro-ness and has been emulated by many current artists, such as Kanye West. MJ's original 'Thriller' jacket was sold at auction for a thrilling $1.8 million, and has been called the 'greatest item of rock and roll memorabilia in history'.

MODERN VINTAGE

'It is only the modern that ever becomes old-fashioned.'

Oscar Wilde, Irish writer and poet

BALL S**T

The World's Biggest Ball of Twine is one of the weirdest – and most pointless – feats ever achieved by human beings. It's also a huge visual reminder of the strangeness of the human psyche.

I mean, what's the point?

Anyway, the World's Biggest Ball of Twine ever built by a community of people was started by Cawker City, Kansas resident Frank Stoeber in 1953. Our Frank had rolled 1.6 million feet (490,000m) of twine on his 11ft- (3.4m-) diameter ball before he sadly passed away in 1974.

Though the story doesn't end there.

The crazy residents of Cawker City went on to build an open-air gazebo around Stoeber's ball, and now every August a 'Twine-a-thon' is held and local residents add more twine to the ball.

By 2006 – the last time anyone checked I presume – the twine ball had reached a weight of 17,886lb (8,111kg), with a staggering circumference of 40ft (12m).

How retro is that?

KNITLYMPIAN

Hazel Tindall from the Shetland Islands, off the coast of Scotland, is the fastest knitter in the world – she is a knitlympian, if such a word were to exist.

Hazel won the world speed knitting championship with an epilepsy-inducing speed of 262 stitches in three minutes.

However, she is not recognized by the Guinness World Records as the world's fastest knitter, as they were not present to officiate Hazel's record-making attempt. The current record for the world's fastest knitter is held by Miriam Tegels from Holland. When asked if Hazel would attempt her record again for Guinness, Hazel replied 'no' as it would be 'a lot of faff'.

BEYOND RETRO

Opening near the infamous and rather smelly Brick Lane in East London in 2002, Beyond Retro was named number nine in *Time Out London*'s '50 best shops in London'. The shop is recognized as one of London's premier retro outlets, and the brand itself boasts that they are 'fast becoming a vintage legend – an innovative retailer with a rock and roll heart' and 'as the vintage vision is brought to more people across the world with its internationally available online store, Beyond Retro retains its original cultural essence with the nostalgia that's intrinsic to the Beyond Retro world.'

So, it's basically a shop that sells smelly, old clothes on a smelly street in smelly London.

BIG JOHNSON

The international truth-sayer, as well as popular environmentalist, melodic singer-songwriter and all around nice guy, Jack Johnson, went to extraordinary lengths to show us all how on-trend he really is when it comes to living in the materialist, over-the-counter culture we all hate really. He wrote a song with some pretty special lyrics.

'The Three R's' by Jack Johnson (selected lyrics)

We've got to learn to
Reduce, Reuse, Recycle
If you're going to the market to buy some juice
You've got to bring your own bags and you learn to reduce your
waste
And if your brother or your sister's got some cool clothes
You could try them on before you buy some more of those

LICENCE TO BUNT

Bunting is so trendy at the moment it even got a sneaky little mention in 2012's *Skyfall* – James Bond's most recent outing, directed by Sam Mendes. It comes towards the end of the movie when M (played by Judi Dench) is being drilled on her job performance. I believe this is the first ever time in the history of language that the words 'bunting' and 'dead operatives' appear in the same statement.

M: Well, I'm not saying it's all gone perfectly, but …
Clair Dowar MP: You'll forgive me for not putting up the bunting. I find it rather difficult to overlook the monumental security breaches and dead operatives for which you are almost single-handedly responsible.

ANTIQUES ROADSHOW

If you affix the word 'vintage', 'antique' or 'retro' to some objects you can instantly increase their value by about a million per cent, although this is not always the case. Take a look at these cost projections I've put together (i.e. made up) for some items in Britain and you can see how out-of-control the vintage market can get.

	VALUE NOW (£)	RETRO VALUE IN 20 YEARS (£)
Vintage car	5,000	20,000
Decent bottle of wine	7.99	150
Leather jacket	150	2
Fur coat	20,000	70
Wedding dress	8,000	50
Engagement rings	2,000	500
Wooden chair	200	10,000

READY STEADY RETRO

In 1920s America, prohibition was all the rage. Literally. Most of the country was very angry about it. Drinking alcohol was illegal. There was an upside, however. Many code words for alcohol started to spring up to disguise the fact that you were no longer going to go to a 'bar' to get 'drunk'. You were now attending 'speakeasies' to get 'spifficiated' on 'bootleg'.

Here are some other 1920s-period code words for alcohol that are still in use today.

Tanked

Canned

Razzed

Sloshed

Corked

Scrooched

Jazzed

Zozzled

Gibbered

Gunned

Pickled

Honkeyed

Plastered

Hootered

Lathered

Buzzed

Squiffy

Primed

Blasted

Blootered

Blottoed

Tiddly

Trousered

Walloped

ACKNOWLEDGMENTS

I'd like to apologise to my editor Katie Hewett – she told me a million times my hyperbole was horrible and I never listened. A massive shout out (to use modern vernacular) must also go to the team at Portico Books.

A NOTE ON SOURCES

www.allaboutyou.com; archive.tobacco.org; www.babble.com; www.blumoonevent.com; www.buzzfeed.com; www2.craftandhobby.org; www.craftscounciluk.org.uk; www.dailymail.co.uk; Dallas Morning News; www.dummies. com; www.english-for-students.com; www.environment-agency. gov.uk; fleamarket.org; www.guardian.co.uk; harmony1.com; www.huffingtonpost.com; www.iknit.org.uk; magazine.foxnews. com; www.mbaonline.com; www.narts.org; news.yahoo.com; www.nme.com; www.raptisrarebooks.com; www.resource.uk.com; www.rsi-therapy.com; www.smokingstatistics.org; www.soyouwanna.com; www.telegraph.co.uk; theairspace.net; www.thesmokingjacket. com; www.thisismoney.co.uk; www.trendhunter.com; www.ukhandknitting.com; www.urbandictionary.com; www.u-s-history.com; waste360.com; www.wikipedia.org; www.wrap.org.uk

First published in the United Kingdom in 2013 by
Portico Books
10 Southcombe Street
London
W14 0RA

An imprint of Anova Books Company Ltd

ISBN 9781909397200

A CIP catalogue record for this book is available from the
British Library.

10 9 8 7 6 5 4 3 2 1

Printed and bound by 1010 Printing International Ltd, China

This book can be ordered direct from the publisher by
www.anovabooks.com